JOBS AROUND THE WORLD

By Mary Pat Ehmann

Gareth Stevens
PUBLISHING

Please visit our website, www.garethstevens.com. For a free color catalog of all our high-quality books, call toll free 1-800-542-2595 or fax 1-877-542-2596.

Library of Congress Cataloging-in-Publication Data

Names: Ehmann, Mary Pat, author.
Title: Jobs around the world / Mary Pat Ehmann.
Description: New York : Gareth Stevens Publishing, [2019] | Series: Adventures in culture | Includes index.
Identifiers: LCCN 2018000113| ISBN 9781538218716 (library bound) | ISBN 9781538218730 (pbk.) | ISBN 9781538218747 (6 pack)
Subjects: LCSH: Job hunting–Juvenile literature.
Classification: LCC HF5382.7 .E397 2019 | DDC 331.702–dc23
LC record available at https://lccn.loc.gov/2018000113

Published in 2019 by
Gareth Stevens Publishing
111 East 14th Street, Suite 349
New York, NY 10003

Copyright © 2019 Gareth Stevens Publishing

Designer: Katelyn E. Reynolds
Editor: Meta Manchester

Photo credits: Cover, p. 1 humphery/Shutterstock.com; pp. 2–24 (background texture) Flas100/Shutterstock.com; p. 5 (teacher) ESB Professional/Shutterstock.com; p. 5 (firefighters) SanchaiRat/Shutterstock.com; p. 5 (vet) didesign021/Shutterstock.com; p. 7 Gordon Bell/Shutterstock.com; p. 9 Rawpixel.com/Shutterstock.com; p. 11 Matt Ragen/Shutterstock.com; p. 13 Fotos593/Shutterstock.com; p. 15 Harry Gerwin/Getty Images; p. 17 Noriko Hayashi/Bloomberg via Getty Images; p. 19 China Photos/Getty Images; p. 21 NASA.

Printed in the United States of America

CPSIA compliance information: Batch #CS18GS: For further information contact Gareth Stevens, New York, New York at 1-800-542-2595.

CONTENTS

Boldface words appear in the glossary.

Job Hunt

Think about your skills and talents. Would they help you be a great firefighter, vet, or teacher someday? People who live in different places may do different jobs. Maybe one of the jobs in this book is just right for you!

Bike Fishermen

In Amsterdam, in the Netherlands, there are many **canals** and about 2 million bicycles. Bikes end up in the water, so there's a special job to get them out! "Bike fishermen" take bikes and other things out of the canals using claw machines.

claw machine

7

Tea-Leaf Pickers

Tea plants are grown all over the world, especially in China, Japan, India, and the United States. Some plants are picked by machine. The best tea is picked by hand! Only the top two leaves and newest leaf bud are used.

tea-leaf picker in Sri Lanka

9

Dabbawalas

In India, a dabbawala (dah-BAH-wah-lah) picks up a meal and delivers it to a person at work. Often, the meal is cooked at the **customer's** home. The dabbawala also returns the empty lunchbox. Dabbawalas usually carry many meals at once.

11

Amazon Rain Forest Guides

The Amazon in South America is the largest **rain forest** in the world. It's home to millions of plants and animals. Amazon guides help others travel safely through the rain forest. They teach others about the people and wildlife that live there.

International Ice Patrol

The US Coast Guard runs the International Ice Patrol (IIP). The IIP follows the movements of **icebergs** using airplanes and computers. It offers ships safe paths around them. If they need to, the IIP tows icebergs out of the way.

tugboat towing an iceberg

Train Pushers

In some countries, many people travel by train to work each day. A person called a pusher helps the people into the train cars! Pushers make sure everyone fits and no one gets hit by a train door.

Panda Caretakers

Giant pandas only live in the wild in China. There are fewer than 2,000 left. The Giant Panda Protection and Research Center in Ya'an, China, is trying to **increase** that number. It **hires** people to be panda caretakers!

Out of This World!

Some people don't work on Earth. They work above it! **Astronauts** and scientists work on the International Space Station. It orbits, or goes around, Earth every 92 minutes! Which job in this book would you like to try?

GLOSSARY

astronaut: someone who works or lives in space

canal: a man-made waterway

customer: someone who buys goods or services

hire: to give work or a job to someone in exchange for money

iceberg: a very large piece of ice floating in the ocean

increase: to become larger in size, amount, or number

rain forest: a forest that gets lots of rain

FOR MORE INFORMATION

BOOKS

Rosen, Michael J., and Ben Kassoy. *Weird Jobs*. Minneapolis, MN: Millbrook Press, 2014.

Squire, Ann. *Extreme Science Careers*. New York, NY: Children's Press, 2015.

Staniford, Linda. *Firefighters to the Rescue Around the World*. Chicago, IL: Heinemann Raintree, 2016.

WEBSITES

Jobs for Kids
www.kidzworld.com/article/23639-jobs-for-kids
Find out about jobs you can do right now!

Science Jobs and Careers
www.sciencekids.co.nz/sciencefacts/careers.html
Read about different jobs in science.

INDEX